D1084915

Hooray for Minnesota Winters!

For Minnesotans (and those who wish they *were*) of All Ages

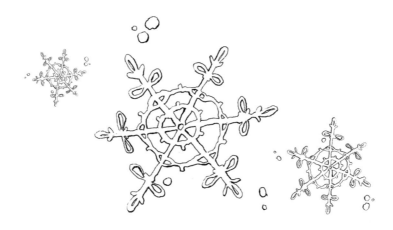

Paul Lowrie and Bret Nicholaus

Edited by **Joe & Jennifer Lindholm** and **Allison Thompson**
Illustrations by **Jennifer Awes**

Warm Words Press
a division of William Randall Publishing

Warm Words Press
a division of William Randall Publishing
P.O. Box 340, Yankton, SD 57078
www.HoorayforMinnesota.com

Illustrations by Jennifer Awes
Graphic design by Ann Lundstrom
www.demo-graphics-design.com

Edited by Joe & Jennifer Lindholm and Allison Thompson

William Randall Publishing's authors are available for seminars and speaking engagements.
If interested please contact us at the address listed above.

ATTENTION: SCHOOLS AND BUSINESSES
William Randall Publishing's books are available at quantity discounts
with bulk purchase for educational, business, or promotional use.
For more information, contact:
William Randall Publishing, Special Sales Department,
P.O. Box 340, Yankton, SD 57078

ISBN #978-0-9755801-9-6

Printed in Korea

First Edition: October 2005
Second Edition: October 2008

10 9 8 7 6 5 4 3 2 1

Hooray for Minnesota Winters!

For Minnesotans (and those who wish they *were*) of All Ages

All temperatures listed in this book are in Fahrenheit.

A FEW COMMENTS
FROM THE
CREW

Minnesota in wintertime: the cold, the snow, the ice, the wind, the length of the season…. Ahhh, but we love it all, don't we? Well, O.K., maybe we don't *love* everything about winter, but we certainly tolerate the season extremely well! And if an "outsider" happens to ask us about our winters, we're all-too-ready to exaggerate—just a wee bit—how cold it gets, how much snow piles up, and how very, very long the winters last. We love to talk about how hard winters build endurance, and endurance builds character (in fact, we're a whole state *full* of characters, aren't we?). We're also glad to point out all the fun and unusual activities Minnesotans do in winter, like ice-fish for gross, carnivorous things known as eelpout! Outsiders think we're absolutely nuts; we, of course, know that we're perfectly normal.

At any rate, this entertaining book deals with both the fact and fiction of our "favorite" season. As is the case when listening to any Minnesotan weave a tale of winter, it is at times hard to tell in this poem where the facts begin and the fiction ends—but that's exactly what makes descriptions of Minnesota winters so much fun. (We should note that wherever you see the words "The Cold Facts," be assured that the truth has not at all been stretched—facts are facts.) Whether you are a Minnesotan or, well, something else, it is our sincere hope that this A-to-Z collection of Minnesota wintertime rhymes gives you many smiles and laughs—and brings to mind some memories of character-building seasons gone by. Enjoy the book, and as always, enjoy the winter!

Paul, Bret, Joe, Jennifer and Allison

How wholesome winter is,
seen far or near.

—Henry David Thoreau (1817-1862)
AMERICAN WRITER AND PHILOSOPHER

FOR GRANT

"A" is for **Alberta** clippers

that swing on *down*

And drop several inches

of snow on our **ground**.

THE **COLD** FACTS

We hear the term numerous times each winter, but what exactly *is* an Alberta clipper? Well, the National Weather Service defines it as "a fast-moving low-pressure system that moves southeast out of the Canadian province of Alberta, and continues through the Plains, Midwest, and Great Lakes region, usually during the winter. It is generally accompanied by light snow, strong winds, and colder temperatures. Another variation of the same system is known as a Saskatchewan Screamer." It's way more than you need to know, but now you know!

"B" is for Broomball,

a Minnesota *thing*;

A broom, ball, and bandages

are all you need to **bring**.

THE COLD FACTS

The game of broomball actually originated in Canada during the early 1900's, but Minnesota is probably correct in touting that it was the first state in our country to really get behind it in a big way—and it seems very safe to say that our state is still the most passionate about it. Having said that, the national organization known as USA Broomball now has many states that it counts as members—including Minnesota, Colorado, New York and Michigan—with more states planning to join in the near future. As for playing the sport on an indoor ice rink, some of the fastest-growing areas for young broomball programs include California, Texas and Florida. Even foreign countries, like Australia, Italy, Hong Kong and Japan, are getting "swept up" in the broomball hype.

"C" is for Cold,

and Colder, and *Coldest*;

When it comes to braving the winter,

Minnesotans are boldest!

THE COLD FACTS

Just how cold is our largest city compared to the most populated areas of our Midwestern neighbors? Let's put it this way: We win! (And to think that Chicagoans talk about how very COLD they get in the winter!) Listed below are the average January high/low temperatures for Minneapolis and other major cities in nearby states:

#8: Indianapolis: 34/18°	#5: Des Moines: 29/12°	#2: Minneapolis: 22/4°
#7: Detroit: 33/20°	#4: Milwaukee: 27/13°	**#1: Warroad, MN: 12/-10°**
#6: Chicago: 32/18°	#3: Green Bay: 24/7°	

We realize that Warroad is not a major city (population 1,682) and that if you went a few miles farther north you'd be in Canada (eh?), but we thought it would be another fun point of comparison.

"D" is for Dreaming

ahead to the Fourth of *July*

When it just might reach

60 degrees for the **high**!

THE COLD FACTS

O.K., let's be honest—it *can* get warmer than 60° on Independence Day. In Bemidji, MN, for example, the average July 4th high temperature is 78°. But consider this: In Paul Bunyan Land, it has never been warmer than 91° for our nation's birthday, and in 1967 the temperature plummeted to 37° for that date. Water-skiing with earmuffs on? Only in Minnesota!

"E" is for Everything

our winter *delivers*—

Snow, ice, and wind...

and oodles of shivers.

THE COLD FACTS

Regardless of where we live in the state, some winters definitely stand out more than others. The five heaviest seasonal snowfall totals recorded in the Twin Cities since official records began in 1884 (the average is around 45"):

#5: 1991-92—84.1"	#3: 1950-51—88.9"	**#1: 1983-84—98.6"**
#4: 1916-17—84.9"	#2: 1981-82—95.0"	

"F" is for Florida,

where they all think we're *crazy*

For living where it's zero

when we could live where it's **eighty**!

THE **COLD** FACTS

Average January high/low in **St.Cloud, MN**: 19/-1°
Average January high/low in **Miami, FL**: 73/63°

On January 9th of 1977, St. Cloud recorded an all-time low of -43°. By contrast, Miami's all-time low temperature is 27°, recorded on February 3rd of 1917 (one can only imagine the panic that must have seized Floridians on that occasion!). It's interesting to note that it isn't until April 5th each year that the average overnight-low temperature in St. Cloud climbs *above* 27°!

RRRRR

"G" is for Groan,

the eerie sound the ice *makes*

As it thickens and hardens

on our 10,000 lakes.

THE COLD FACTS

We're called the "Land of 10,000 Lakes," but truth be told, how many lakes are there in the state? Taking into account all Minnesota lakes that are 10 acres or larger and have a wave-swept shoreline (two of the standards used by the state's DNR to define a lake), there are 11,842—covering 3.3 million acres! That's a lot of water to brag about in the summer, and lots and lots of ice to be proud of in the winter.

"H" is for Hockey,

a sport that we *love*;

To put it quite simply,

we can't get **enough**!

THE COLD FACTS

Considering how immensely popular the sport of hockey is in our state, it would be great if we could truthfully say that the game had its origin here. As most of us know, however (even if we'll never admit it), Minnesota is not its birthplace...nor is Canada! Most sports historians claim that the earliest form of the winter game began about 500 years ago on frozen ponds in Britain and France. Given that fact, it shouldn't surprise us that the word "hockey" likely got its name from a French word, "hoquet," which translates to "shepherd's crook" or "bent stick."

"I" is for **Ice-fishing**

out on the *lake*

While hearing tall tales

from Great Uncle **Jake**.

THE **COLD** FACTS

Walker, Minnesota. Leech Lake. Winter. If you're a Minnesotan, you probably know where we're headed: the annual international Eelpout Festival. For more than 25 years, as many as 10,000 people from around the state, the country, and even the world (including England and Nepal) have come each frigid February to attempt to catch, or watch someone catch, the biggest eelpout. For those who don't know, the eelpout is a disgusting-looking, snake-like, carnivorous, nocturnal codfish that tends to be more active—and thus easier to catch—in the colder months. Thankfully, it tastes quite a bit better than it looks (especially in winter, when its flesh is more firm). Averaging a bit more than 5 pounds each, the largest 'pout caught in the last few years of the famous three-day festival was 14.62 pounds. We know that the anglers catch a lot of fish at this thing (730 in 2007), but do they catch a lot of colds, too?

"J" is for January

and toughing it *out*;

Four feet of snow,

that's what *I'm* talkin' **about**!

THE **COLD** FACTS

Four feet of snow in a month is one thing, but four feet of snow in a couple of days? That's exactly what happened near Finland, MN, in 1994. Between January 6th and the 8th, a raging winter storm dumped 46.5" of snow on the ground there—a single-storm record for the state of Minnesota!

"K" is for Kindling

to get fires *going*;

You're all toasty warm

while outside it's **snowing**.

THE COLD FACTS

...and it kept snowing, and snowing, and snowing. Before dawn on December 6th, 1969, it began to snow in Minneapolis. Apparently the snow took a liking to the city, because it decided to hang around and keep right on snowing until dinnertime on December 9th. This 88-hour span of time marks the longest continuous snowfall ever recorded in the Minneapolis area. Ironically, the total accumulation over that lengthy period was relatively low, just 14".

"L" is for Long,

as in long *underwear*;

If you don't want to freeze,

you put on a **pair**.

THE COLD FACTS

Some all-time record-low temperatures for different parts of the state:

Bloomington: -34°   East Grand Forks: -42°
Mankato: -35°   Ely: -45°
Duluth: -39°   International Falls: -46°
Rochester: -40°   Bemidji: -50°
Willmar: -41°   Brainerd: -54°

Tower, MN, lays claim to the all-time lowest temperature recorded in the state: -60°!

"M" is for Mall of America,

a fun place to *be*

When the windchill outside

is **minus 33**!

THE COLD FACTS

The coldest windchill ever recorded in the vicinity of the Mall of America was back on January 22nd, 1936—long before the world-famous, 520-store Mall arrived! On that date, the windchill in "the Cities" hit -87°. The formula for calculating the windchill changed in 2001, so they now say that the windchill on that January day was probably "only" -67°. Due to sketchy statewide wind records, it is a bit more difficult to pinpoint the all-time coldest windchill in Minnesota. However, on January 9th and 10th of 1982, spots in Northern Minnesota reported temperatures of -30° with winds around 40 mph. Using the new formula, that would translate to a windchill of -71°—a serious contender for the all-time coldest windchill in the state.

"N" is for Never,

as in never *admit*

That the winter gets to you,

not one single **bit**!

THE COLD FACTS

In 1991, winter might have been wearing just a bit thin on the good folks in Duluth by the time they got to, well, winter! During meteorological fall of that year (September, October, November), the city received 56.8" of snow—a 130-year record for those people on the shore of Lake Superior.

"O" is for Over

and Over and Over *again*

We embrace the winter

and call it our friend.

THE **COLD** FACTS

During the winter of 1930-31, the people living in Minneapolis-St. Paul didn't have much of a winter to embrace. That was the season that had the lowest snowfall total in the history of Twin Cities weather records. How much fell? 14.2", a truly paltry and laughable amount by Minnesota standards.

"P" is for Parka,

but also for *Plow*.

Survive winter without them?

No way, no **how**!

THE COLD FACTS

Where would we be without all those plows? In a ditch, for one thing! Thankfully, the Minnesota Department of Transportation has 850 plows that it can send out to keep the state highways and interstates clear of snow and ice. In addition to those hundreds of state-owned plows, the counties and cities around the state have their own fleets. For example, our capital city has roughly 80 plows that it will put into action to clear the local streets during a snow emergency. That means St. Paul has one plow for every 3,550 residents—a phenomenal ratio for any city its size!

"Q" is for Quick,

the best word that *describes*

The length of our summer

once winter subsides.

THE COLD FACTS

Minnesotans know just how short the summer can be...but how do we compare to other locations around the country? We chose Brainerd, MN, as the benchmark for this one.

Number of days each year with an average daytime high temperature of 80° or higher:

Brainerd, MN: 45 (July 2nd through August 15th)
Denver, CO: 93 (June 8th through September 8th)
Charlotte, NC: 133 (May 16th through September 25th)
Phoenix, AZ: 211 (April 4th through October 31st)
Orlando, FL: 238 (March 20th through November 12th)
Honolulu, HI: 361 (January 1st through December 27th)

"R" is for **Ready** to Relax

on some Caribbean *sand*;

We do love our winters,

but how much snow can one **stand**?

THE **COLD** FACTS

In the winter season of 1949-50, 170.5" of snow fell in Grand Portage, an all-time single-season record for Minnesota. On March 28th of 1950, 75" of snow was measured on the ground there—the maximum snow depth ever recorded in the state. By that point, there may have been a *few* people ready to exchange their snow shovels for sand shovels.

GULF OF

MEXICO

FLORIDA

NORTH ATLANTIC
OCEAN

CUBA

HAITI /DOMINICAN
REPUBLIC

US/BRITISH
VIRGIN
ISLANDS

PUERTO
RICO

JAMAICA

ANTIGUA

ST. KITTS

CARIBBEAN SEA

DOMINICA

MARTINIQUE

ST. LUCIA

BARBADOS

"S" is for St. Paul,

with its Winter Carnival each *year*;

A carnival for *winter*?

Minnesotans say, "Here, Here!"

THE COLD FACTS

When a New York reporter wrote in 1885 that St. Paul was "another Siberia, unfit for human habitation," it demanded an appropriate response from the St. Paul Chamber of Commerce. Thus, the Saint Paul Winter Carnival made its debut in 1886, proving to those thin-skinned New Yorkers that not only was St. Paul habitable, but its people could actually *celebrate* the cold and snow. As is still the case in certain years, that first carnival featured an elaborate ice castle made from the frozen water of Minnesota lakes (1992 was the year that featured the largest ice castle ever built in the world—150 feet high). The 10-day festival includes such events as parades, coronations, concerts, ice-carving contests, and the famous Softball on Ice Tournament. In a typical year, roughly 250,000 people gladly brave the mid-winter cold and enjoy the carnival.

"T" is for Tubing

down a steep, icy *hill*;

Throw in some trees

and you've got quite a **thrill**!

THE COLD FACTS

There are plenty of good tubing days available to every Minnesotan. For example, tubers in Bloomington can do their thing 100 days a year—that's the average number of days with 1" or more of snow on the ground in that part of the state. Farther north, we measure snow depth by the *foot*: In Ely, for example, roughly 80 days each year have at least 12" of snow on the ground!

41

"U" is for

"Up der in Dulut'

de sure get da *snow*!"

(We talk a bit differ'nt in Minnesohda,

don' cha **know**.)

THE **COLD** FACTS

No matter how you speak, you're telling the truth when you say that Duluth can get substantial amounts of the white stuff! Even in a normal year, its airport records 83" of snow. The five snowiest seasons in the city's history since 1875:

#5: 1988-89—119.1"	#3: 1996-97—127.9"	**#1: 1995-96—135.4"**
#4: 1968-69—121.0"	#2: 1949-50—131.6"	

"V" is for Vroom!

that exhilarating *sound*

That a snowmobile makes

as it zips you **around**.

THE **COLD** FACTS

The first commercial snowmobiles made in the U.S. were manufactured in Minnesota in 1953. Nowadays, 1 out of every 20 people in the state owns a snowmobile...that's a lot of vrooming!

A note to fellow football fans: Yes, "V" is ALSO for Vikings; but since most of the football schedule is actually played in the fall, we opted to choose something different (and less predictable) here. We hope you can forgive us. Go Vikes!

"W" is for Winter,

and let's be perfectly *clear*:

If it weren't for July and August,

it would last the whole year!

THE COLD FACTS

Accumulating snow has fallen in International Falls as early as mid-September, and in the northern town of Mizpah (not to be confused with Mazeppa in the southern part of the state), 1.5" of snow has fallen as late as June 4th. As far south as the Cities, the month of May has brought at least 3" of snow on three different occasions.

One of the biggest snowstorms in state history began in October: By the time the 1991 "Halloween Blizzard" ceased on November 3rd, 28.4" of snow had fallen at the Minneapolis-St. Paul International Airport—the largest single-snowstorm total in Twin Cities history. Other places in the state received upwards of three feet of snow from the same late-October system!

As for temperatures, we can't even count on August to keep us above freezing. Many places in the state have posted August readings in the 20s, but Cass Lake holds the record for the month: On August 1st, 1952, the town recorded a temperature of (drum roll, please) 20°! Would you like lemonade or hot chocolate with your barbequed chicken?

"X" marks the spot—

International Falls;

In all the U.S.,

it can be the coldest of all!

THE COLD FACTS

On nightly winter weather forecasts around the nation, International Falls often receives mention—and for good reason. Their average January high/low is 14/-8°; from January 6-22 the average overnight low reaches -9°; and from December 12th through February 17th—a span of 68 days—the average overnight low never rises above 0°! In addition to the cold, International Falls residents have to contend each year with the roughly 70" of snow that comes their way.

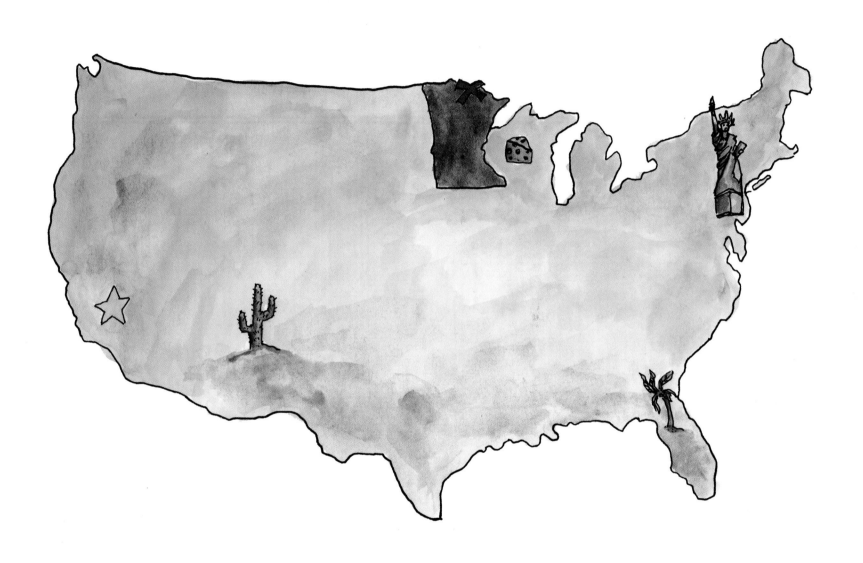

"Y" is for "Yah, sure!" and "Ya betcha!"

which is what a Minnesotan might *say*

If somebody asked him if 20 degrees

was a warm winter **day**.

THE COLD FACTS

After a prolonged period of near- or sub-zero weather, 20° can indeed feel balmy to a Minnesotan! But just how warm *has* it gotten in the dead of winter? Some all-time January highs for cities around the state:

Duluth: 47°	Moorhead: 53°	St. Paul: 57°
Hibbing: 48°	East Grand Forks: 54°	Owatonna: 58°
Baudette: 50°	St. Cloud: 56°	Winona: 64°

The state record for the month of January belongs to Springfield, where on January 25th, 1981, it reached a whopping 67°!

"**Z**" is for **Zero,**

and it's not just a *temp*;

It's the number of wintertime

rhymes that are **left**.

Though the rhyming is over,

winter's still *here*;

So go out, have a ball,

and be of good **cheer**!

The greater part of our happiness depends on our dispositions,
and not our circumstances.

—*Martha Washington*

THREE **EASY-TO-FOLLOW**
SETS OF WINTER INSTRUCTIONS
FOR **NON-MINNESOTANS**

(It wouldn't be fair to keep all the secrets to ourselves!)

How to make a snow-angel:

1. Lie down in the snow, facing skyward.

2. Move arms and legs back and forth in a jumping-jack motion.

3. Carefully stand up and admire the design.

Note: As snow melts, design will fade away.

How to make a snowball:

1. Collect some snow in the palms of your hands.

2. Squeeze snow tightly in your hands until it forms a solid ball.

3. Pull arm back and release the snowball toward your target.

Note: Heavy, wet snow is easier to pack than fluffy, dry snow.

How to make hot chocolate:

1. Heat some milk in a pan on the stove.

2. Pour carefully into a heat-resistant mug.

3. Add chocolate syrup or powder, stir well, and drink.

Note: Sip slowly at first, as hot liquids can burn your mouth.

WORDS
OF
THANKS & CREDITS

Thanks to the following organizations and websites for providing us with the facts and statistics listed in this book: National Oceanic and Atmospheric Administration (NOAA), National Weather Service, The Weather Channel, Minnesota Climatology Office, Duluth Weather Office, Minnesota Department of Tourism, Minnesota Department of Natural Resources (DNR), Minnesota Department of Transportation, City of St. Paul, City of Minneapolis, Walker, MN, Chamber of Commerce, *Outdoors Weekly, Chicago Tribune*, Minnesota Sports Federation, the NHL®, winter-carnival.com, northlandconnection.com, broomball.com, usabroomball.com, and all the kind people that took time to answer our unusual questions.

ABOUT THE AUTHORS & EDITORS

PAUL LOWRIE was born in St. Louis Park, Minnesota. His family moved to South Dakota when he was 10, but Lowrie returned to his home state to attend Bethel University in St. Paul. Since graduating in 1991, he has lived and worked in both Minnesota and South Dakota.

BRET NICHOLAUS is a 1991 graduate of Bethel University (where he met Paul Lowrie and Joe Lindholm). Though he, his wife and their son live in his home state of Illinois, they often return to Minnesota to vacation and visit close friends.

JOE & JENNIFER LINDHOLM are life-long residents of Minnesota and currently live in Brainerd with their two young boys. **ALLISON THOMPSON** was born and raised in Paynesville, Minnesota, and is a 2004 graduate of Concordia College in Moorhead.

ABOUT THE DESIGNER

ANN LUNDSTROM was born and raised in Sioux Falls, South Dakota. Since graduating from the University of South Dakota in 2004 with a degree in graphics and multimedia, she has poured her creative energies into growing her graphic and web design business. Ann, her husband, and their twin son and daughter live in Hawarden, Iowa. The Lundstroms frequently visit family in the Minneapolis/St. Paul area.

ABOUT
THE
ILLUSTRATOR

JENNIFER AWES was born in Lansing, Michigan, and grew up in northwestern Wisconsin. In 1999 she moved to St. Paul to attend Bethel University. She and her husband recently moved from Minnesota to Connecticut, where Jennifer is studying visual art and religion at Yale University.